Babies

Jenny Wood

Photographs by Maggie Murray
Illustrations by Sheila Jackson

A & C Black · London

Published by A & C Black (Publishers) Limited
35 Bedford Row
London WC1R 4JH
This edition © 1991 A & C Black (Publishers) Limited

ISBN 0 7136 3353 0

A CIP catalogue record for this book
is available from the British Library.

Apart from any fair dealing for the purposes of research or
private study, or criticism or review, as permitted under the
Copyright, Designs and Patents Act, 1988, this publication
may be reproduced, stored or transmitted, in any form or by
any means, only with the prior permission in writing of the
publishers, or in the case of reprographic reproduction in
accordance with the terms of licences issued by the Copyright
Licensing Agency. Inquiries concerning reproduction outside
those terms should be sent to the publishers at the above
named address.

Filmset by August Filmsetting, Haydock, St Helens
Printed in Italy by Amadeus

Contents

A baby is born	4
Time-line	6
Welcoming the new baby	8
Another mouth to feed	9
Baby's layette	10
Time for a feed	13
Bottle feeding	14
Weaning	16
Who's looking after baby?	17
Nannies and nurseries	18
Exercise	20
Keeping baby clean	22
Orphans and foundlings	24
Poor little mite	26
'A fit and virile race'	28
How to find out more	30
Places to visit	31
Index	32

A baby is born

How much do you know about your own birth? Is there an interesting family story about your birthday? Were you born at home or in a hospital?

Nowadays, most parents go to ante-natal classes to find out what will happen and what they will have to do when their baby is born. They can choose to have their babies in hospital and, in Britain, they don't have to pay for medical care.

Mothers can ask for anaesthetics to help stop pain during birth and they know that if there is a problem, highly trained medical staff are on hand to help. Fathers can watch the birth and may even take photographs.

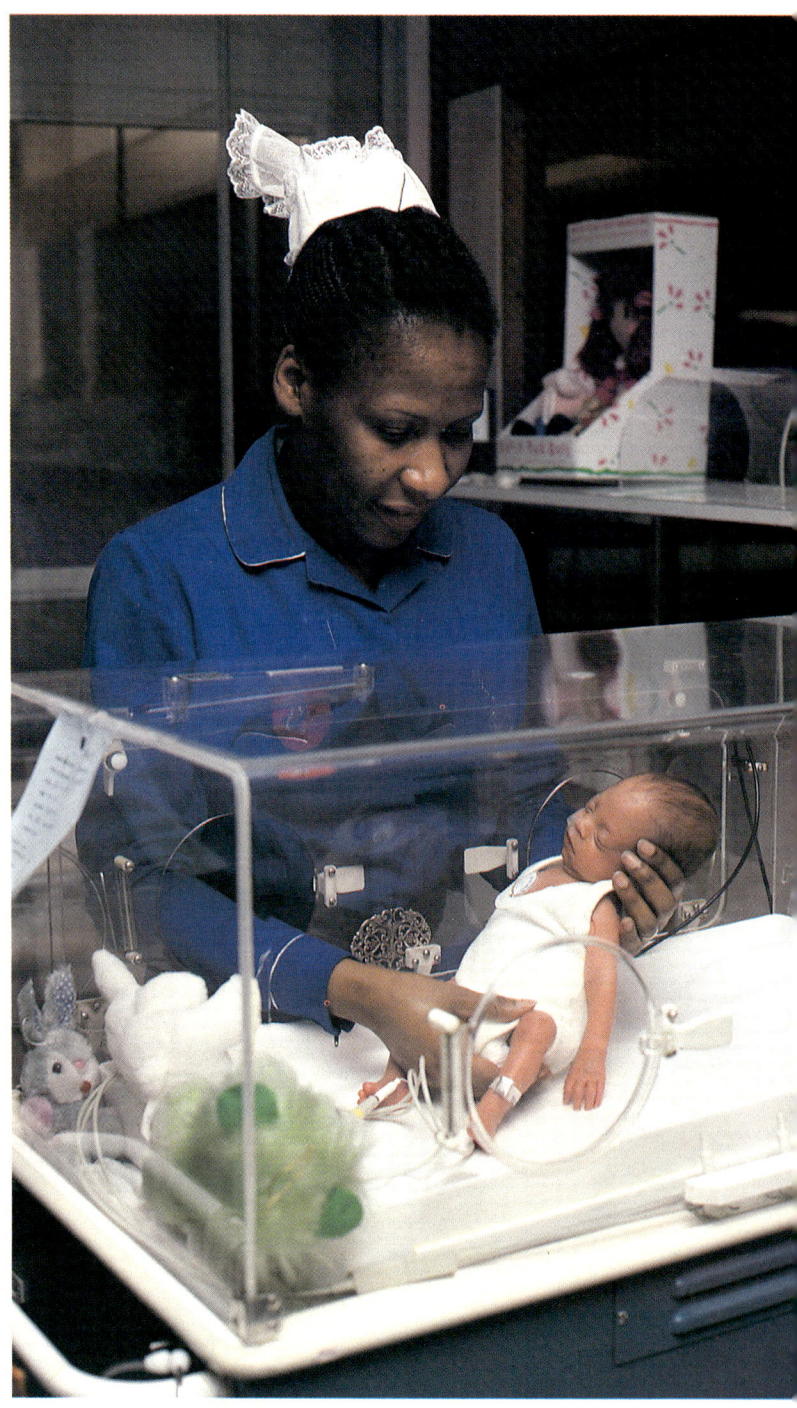

▲ A premature baby being put into an incubator. In a modern, well-equipped hospital, and looked after by skilled doctors and nurses, it has an excellent chance of survival.

▼ These children talked to relatives and neighbours to find out about babies at the turn of the century.

▼ This photo from an album shows a family in 1912. The average number of children at this time was six, but families with twelve or more were quite common.

A hundred years ago, birth was a very different experience. Most mothers had their babies at home. If the mother was rich, she was helped by a doctor and a midwife. If she was poor, she was more likely to be helped by a neighbour with no medical training.

Anaesthetics were not widely available. Most women were given gin to dull the pain. If there were complications, the baby probably died. One out of five babies died at birth, and of those who survived, one in four died within a year.

Time-line

	pre-1880s	1880s	1890s	1900s	1910s	1920s
		Great great grandparents were born		**Great grandparents were born**		
Important events	**1870** Alexander Graham Bell invents telephone	**1888** Dunlop invents pneumatic tyre	**1890** Moving pictures start **1896** First modern Olympic Games	**1901** Queen Victoria dies. Edward VII becomes King **1903** Wright brothers fly first plane	**1910** George V becomes King **1914–18** World War I	**1926** General Strike in Britain
Babies dates	**1848** First Public Health Act **1849** Safety pin invented by Walter Hunt **1850s** Vaccination against smallpox becomes compulsory for children **1860** Pasteurisation of milk is discovered by Louis Pasteur **1862** Refrigeration is invented. This made the storage of baby food much safer	**1880** 45 mothers die per 10 000 births **1889** NSPCC (National Society for the Prevention of Cruelty to Children) is founded	**1891** Factory Act forbade women to work for one month after giving birth. A serum obtained from a horse greatly improved the treatment of diphtheria **1896** Invention of a boat-shaped feeding bottle, named the Allenbury Feeder **1898** Apparatus for pasteurising milk at home became available **1899** First depot for sterilised milk opens in St Helens. It was modelled on one in France	**1900** 154 infant deaths per 1000 births **1902** Midwives Act. It became illegal for unqualified women to call themselves midwives **1903** 40 mothers die per 10 000 births ● First use of the word 'dummy' to describe a baby's comforter **1906** Institution of National Society of Day Nurseries founded to provide day nurseries **1907** First school for mothers opens	**1910** Pregnant women are given financial help for the first time **1915** The first ante-natal clinic established in Edinburgh. From now on all births must be reported to local authorities **1918** Maternity and Child Welfare Act. This allowed authorities to set up clinics for pregnant women **1919** Paediatrics (children's health care) becomes a compulsory subject for trainee doctors and midwives	**1924** Paper tissues introduced ● Vaccine against tuberculosis (T.B.) is developed **1925** 75 infant deaths per 1000 births **1926** The Adoption Act. Adoption became legal in Britain. It had been legalised in USA in 185_ **1929** Chelsea Baby Club founded. This was a middle class version of the School for Mothers

This time-line shows some of the important events since your great grandparents were children, and some of the events and inventions which have changed how babies are delivered and raised.

	randparents were born		Parents were born			You were born	
930s	1940s	1950s	1960s	1970s	1980s	1990s
6 Edward abdicates. rge VI omes King First vision adcasts 9 World r II starts	1941 Penicillin successfully tested 1945 World War II ends 1947 First supersonic plane	1952 Elizabeth II becomes Queen 1959 Yuri Gagarin first man in space	1969 Neil Armstrong first man on the moon	1973 Britain enters the Common Market	1981 First successful space shuttle flight	
s ned baby s in tins ars me ly able antly Read a book Natural birth uraged ers to their s at , with the num of sthetics 64 infant s per births	1941 Penicillin is successfully tested on a human being 1948 National Health Service begins • Register introduced for paid childminders	1950s Dr Spock, an American doctor, encouraged mothers to feed 'on demand' instead of at regular intervals • Natural childbirth becomes more popular again. Dr Leboyer recommends that mother should give birth in a large tank of warm water	1960s More families owned a car. This led to carry cots and baby buggies replacing bulky prams • The contraceptive pill makes family planning much easier • Disposable nappies become popular 1962 Babygro stretch suit invented in New York by Walter Artat	1977 14 infant deaths per 1000 births 1978 First test tube baby	1980s Strong medical evidence points to increased danger of cancer from using the contraceptive pill 1980 Report shows 80% of first-time mothers are breast feeding 1980 1 mother dies per 10 000 births	1990s 'His' and 'Her disposable nappies became popular, instead of on for all

7

Welcoming the new baby

Did your family have a special ceremony to celebrate your birth? Some people put an announcement in the paper, some have religious services such as a christening or naming ceremony.

A hundred years ago, babies who died before they had been christened weren't allowed a proper burial, so parents christened their new babies as quickly as they could.

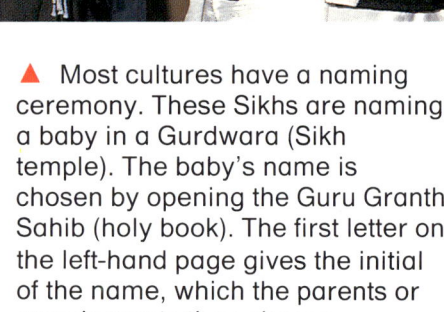

▲ Most cultures have a naming ceremony. These Sikhs are naming a baby in a Gurdwara (Sikh temple). The baby's name is chosen by opening the Guru Granth Sahib (holy book). The first letter on the left-hand page gives the initial of the name, which the parents or grandparents then choose.

If the baby was weak, it was christened almost immediately at the bedside. If the baby was strong, the christening took place later. Rich people often sent out cards announcing the arrival of a new baby, and held magnificent christening parties with dozens of guests. Poorer people had a family party, or went to the pub.

▲ A christening certificate. This one belonged to Doris Cooksley's husband, Walter.

Another mouth to feed

Slum children in 1900.

In Victorian times, the arrival of a baby was often a cause for worry rather than for joy. For most people it meant extra expense and another mouth to feed. Doris Cooksley, who was born in 1900, remembers:

'There were eleven of us children, but two died. I think it must have been a terrible struggle for mother to look after us all.'

Families were much larger than they are now. Planning a family was almost impossible because there were few effective methods of birth control and there was almost no advice on family planning. Mothers often had one baby after another.

▲ A Birth Registration certificate. In 1874 an Act of Parliament made it compulsory for parents to report the birth of a baby to the authorities. The registration certificate proved that they had done so.

As well as looking after a large family, many women had to go back to work immediately after having a baby. Many mothers, worn out and badly nourished, with little medical care, became ill or died in childbirth.

9

Baby's layette

The clothing, toilet articles and bedding needed for a baby are called a layette. Modern parents can buy a huge range of items, specially designed to be safe for the baby and easy to use. Nappies are usually disposable, so they don't have to be washed. Clothing is made from materials such as cotton, which are easy to launder.

At the turn of the century, far less was known about baby care. The items in the layette were often not very convenient to use. Many of the materials we take for granted, such as plastic which is waterproof and easy to wipe clean, had not been invented.

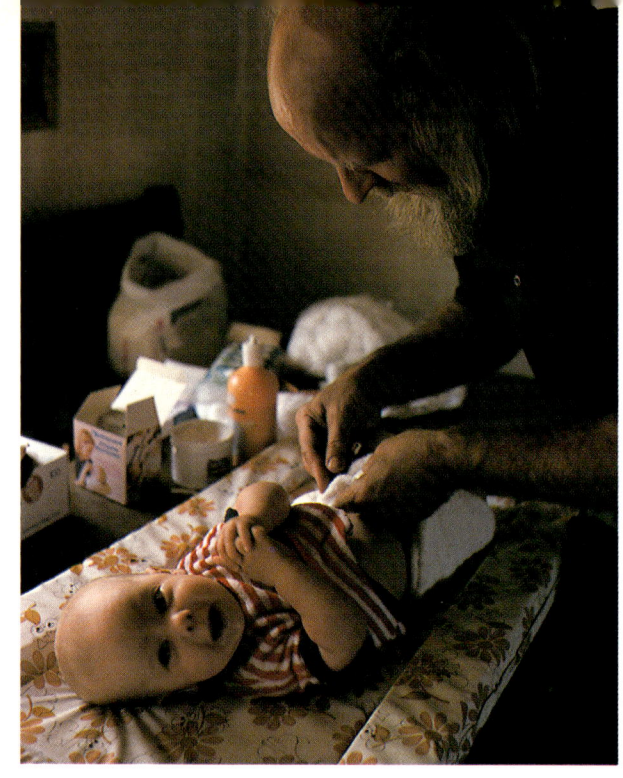

▲ Some items from a modern layette.

▼ This is how one book of advice for mothers written in 1906, described some of the items in an ideal layette. Only a rich family could have afforded all these items.

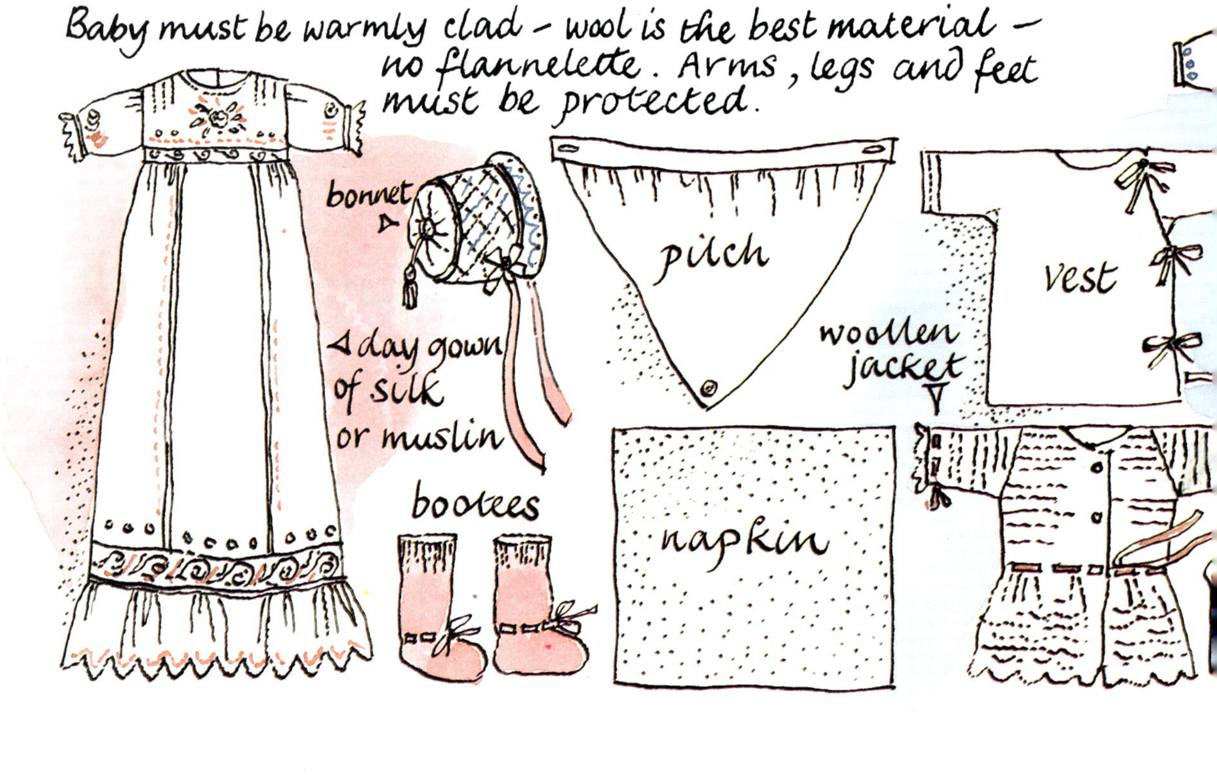

Baby must be warmly clad — wool is the best material — no flannelette. Arms, legs and feet must be protected.

bonnet

day gown of silk or muslin

bootees

pilch

woollen jacket

napkin

vest

▲ Some of the items from a layette at the turn of the century. The photo also shows three china baby feeders, a baby's mug and plate, and a glass feeding bottle.

Shortened at 3 months. Long flannel replaced by woollen drawers buttoned into little bodice of flannel.

bib

binder

Victorian babies wore two sorts of nappies — a soft muslin square placed next to the skin, and a towelling nappy over that. The nappies were folded in half to make triangular shapes of double thickness, and were fastened at the front with a large safety pin. The muslin square protected the baby's delicate skin because, with frequent washing, the towelling nappy became rough.

These nappies were not very absorbent. Many mothers placed a thick piece of flannel, called a pilch, over the nappies at night to help keep the rest of the baby's clothing and bed dry until morning. Some writers on childcare recommended that waterproof oiled silk pilches should be wrapped over the nappies when they were in place. But many people thought that these made mothers or nannies lazy, since they no longer had to change nappies as soon as they became wet.

Poor people could only afford hand-me-downs and rags for their infants, but babies from wealthy families were dressed very elaborately. Keeping baby warm was considered essential, so the infant was wrapped in several layers. Wide strips of flannel or woollen cloth were bound round baby's waist to support its back. The Victorians believed that having wool next to the skin was healthy, so babies wore woollen vests.

On top of the vest, the baby wore one or more long robes, depending on the weather. The robes kept the baby's feet warm and stopped it from crawling easily. The Victorians didn't like their babies crawling, because it reminded them of the ape–like behaviour of their ancestors. Victorian doctors advised mothers to keep their babies' brains warm with knitted caps.

▲ A baby's robe and cap. By the turn of the century most doctors believed that a baby's head should be kept cool, but caps and bonnets were still in use in the 1920s.

▼ This photo, taken about 80 years ago, shows a baby wrapped in its many layers. Boys wore girls' clothes until they were about 3, when they were 'breeched' by being given their first pair of trousers.

Time for a feed

At the start of the Victorian period there was very little scientific knowledge about how babies should be fed. Most mothers preferred breast feeding, which we now know is the best method.

During Victoria's reign, breast feeding became less fashionable amongst middle-class women. Richer mothers who wanted their babies to have breast-milk often employed wet-nurses, women with a good supply of their own milk, to feed their babies.

▲ Wet nurses in action. Many people believed that the character of the nurse could be transmitted through her milk. Red-haired nurses were unpopular in case they passed on a bad temper!

◀ Mother's milk contains exactly the right nourishment for a baby.

Bottle feeding

Bottle feeding became more popular in Queen Victoria's reign. Until the glass baby's bottle arrived from France in 1851, women used a hollowed-out cow's horn fitted with a leather teat to hold the milk. These were difficult to clean, and the germs which collected in them caused diseases. Many of the early glass bottles were just as unhygienic.

At first, babies were fed with untreated cows' milk. This was not very nourishing and often carried diseases.

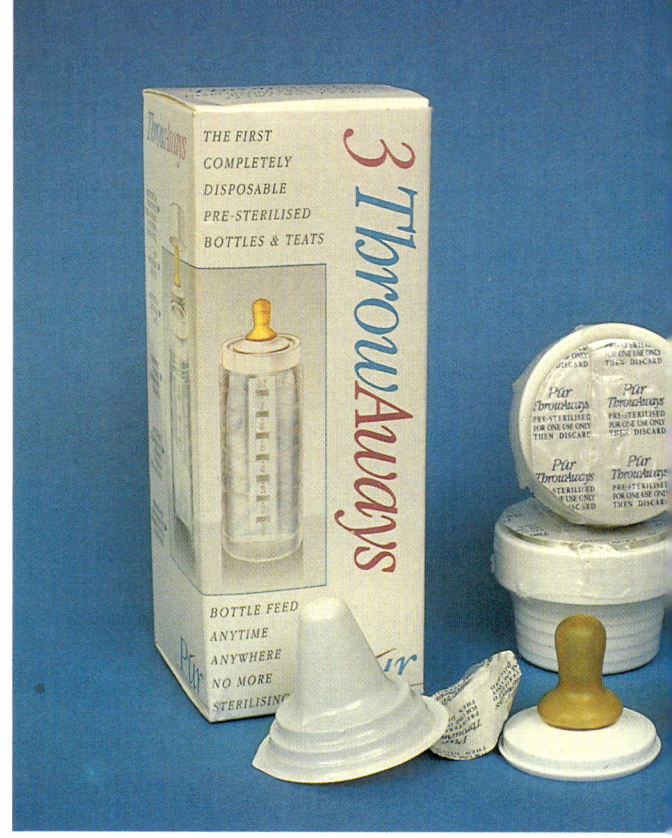

Early feeding bottles were seldom sterilised. The long thin tube, through which the baby sucked the milk, was difficult to clean and became a breeding ground for germs.

◀ Some of the latest babies' bottles. They are packed in sterile wrappings and are thrown away after use.

▼ Later feeding bottles were fitted with washable rubber teats. They were easier to keep clean because they had openings at both ends. A teat was placed on one end and, on the other end, there was a rubber valve which allowed in air as the baby sucked.

1896. Boat Shaped Bottle
Naked. Allenbury Feeder

By 1884 there were 27 different brands of baby 'milk' available. Most contained dried or condensed cow's milk with flour and malt added. No proper advice was given about the amount of water which had to be added, or the amount of food which should be given to a baby. Cheaper brands often came in large tins. What was left in the bottom of an opened tin often went bad before it was used.

Babies raised in orphanages were always bottle fed. In 1880 up to one third of these babies died as a result of contamination of the bottle or their feed. It was not until 1891 that a Dr Goodhart wrote simple and foolproof instructions for the timing and quantities for hand feeding.

After 1900, mothers could buy equipment to ▶ sterilise babies' bottles and milk at home.

Weaning

Before the turn of the century, doctors weren't sure exactly when a baby should be weaned off milk on to more solid food. Some mothers weaned their babies when the first teeth appeared. Many babies were eating meat at six months; their nurses might chew the meat themselves before giving it to the infant.

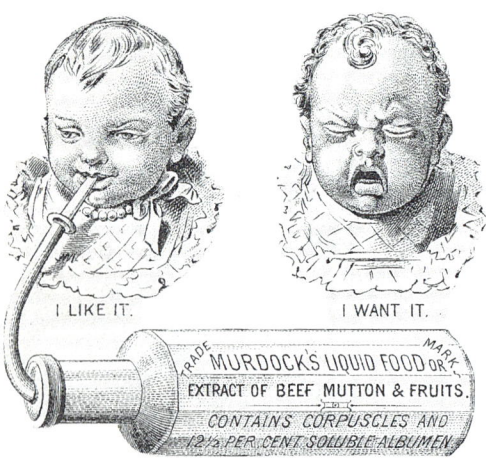

▲ An advertisement for baby food from the turn of the century. Cheap baby foods often contained flour which was hard to digest or cow's milk which lacked essential fats.

These children looked at some modern baby foods. They noticed that the moist foods all came in small jars or tins. Can you think why?

The first solid food, called pap, was a mixture of bread, sugar, water, castor oil, rusks, porridge or arrowroot. It was fed to the baby from a pap boat. Pap boats were often not washed properly and they carried germs which caused diseases.

The pap itself was often missing important vitamins and, as a result, many babies became ill with diseases such as rickets which softened the bones. Poor people who could not afford special baby foods often used unsuitable foods such as watered-down beer.

After 1900 brand names such as Hovis and Robinson's, began to appear. These were scientifically formulated and with proper use, vitamin deficiency diseases and gastro-enteritis became less common.

Who's looking after baby?

Working mothers from poorer families could not afford to employ maids or servants to look after their babies while they were at work. Many carried their babies wherever they went, even to work. In large families older brothers or sisters looked after the baby. These children were kept away from school on washday when mother was busy, or on days when she was away at work.

If there were no older brothers or sisters, mothers often left their babies alone in the house, dosed with Godfrey's Cordial. This was a soothing medicine which contained opium, a dangerous and addictive drug.

▲ In many modern families, fathers help to look after the baby. At the turn of the century the father had almost nothing to do with child rearing.

▼ A slum child looking after his younger brother and sister. What clues can you find in the picture which show you that they are very poor?

17

Nannies and nurseries

Better-off families usually employed a nanny to look after the children. Servants were so badly paid that even modest, middle-class households could afford to employ a nanny. The very wealthy had an army of nannies, nurses, under-nurses, nurse-maids and cleaners to look after their children.

During the 1890s there were probably over 250,000 nannies employed in Britain. Most of them learned their trade by working in a nursery and watching other nannies.

Mrs McIver started as a kitchen maid in a large house in 1905. When nanny needed someone to help her, she went up to the nursery. She remembers:

'When Nanny Duckworth retired I took over as nanny. I didn't have any qualifications, but I stayed on for another ten years.'

▼ These children visited a reconstructed Victorian day nursery in the Cecil Higgins Museum which contains the kind of toys and 'improving' books which were found in nurseries at the turn of the century.

▲ A nursery at the turn of the century. The nurse-maid feeds the infant with a bottle. Nanny is hard at work repairing the children's clothes.

The night nursery. Very young babies often slept in cots beside nanny's bed.

Children spent most of their time in the nursery with nanny. Large households had two nurseries – the night nursery for sleeping and the day nursery, a large airy room where the children spent their time during the day. The furniture was old and shabby, so the children would not damage anything valuable.

Most nannies kept a strict timetable. The day was divided into eating, playing, having lessons and taking exercise.

Nursery food had to be plain and nourishing.

▼ The children found a night light and a stoneware hot water bottle.

Dr Chavasse advised:

'I recommend a great sameness in an infant's diet... mashed potatoes ought to be his staple vegetable... He ought to have a pudding for his dinner – either rice, tapioca, suet-pudding, batter-pudding or Yorkshire pudding'.

Nannies ate with the children in the nursery. They taught the children good manners and their first lessons. When the children were old enough, they were handed over to a governess.

Exercise

▲ When the twins examined this double pushchair they thought that although it was beautifully made, it was probably rather uncomfortable.

▲ A nanny with a perambulator. Many doctors disapproved of this type of pram because the baby could not lie down, and they thought that sitting up damaged the baby's spine.

Most doctors and nannies believed that fresh air was good for babies. Dr Chavasse in *'Advice to Mothers'* recommended:

'In summer, an infant may be taken out when two weeks old; in winter at the end of a month. When once the baby has been taken out of doors let him go out every day. North-easterly and easterly winds are to be avoided. In wet weather, let fun and frolic be in the nursery, with as little use of brain at pictures and books as possible'.

A nanny 'exercised' her baby by taking it for a ride in a perambulator. Public parks were favourite place for nannies to parade their charges.

Few parents played with their children. People didn't realise that babies could learn by playing. Children were expected to be 'seen and not heard'. Many rich parents hardly knew their children, and only saw them when they were brought downstairs by nanny for an hour before bedtime.

Many parents wanted to see their children doing something 'useful' rather than wasting time playing about. Working mothers had little time to play with their babies. Older children did their share of the chores as soon as they could walk. They ran errands and carried messages – an important job in a world with virtually no telephones.

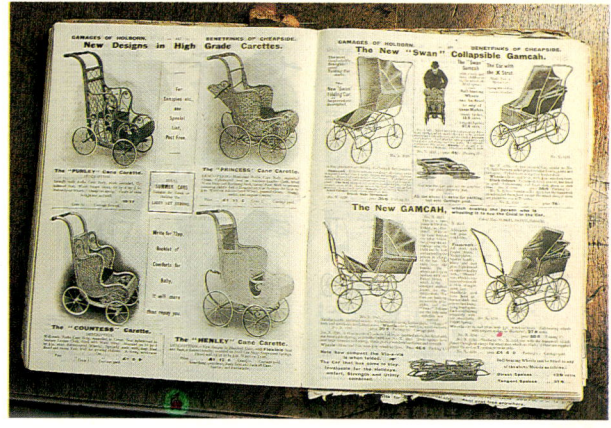

▲ Baby carriages in a mail order catalogue.

▼ Babies' rattles from the turn of the century. The wooden one is probably home-made.

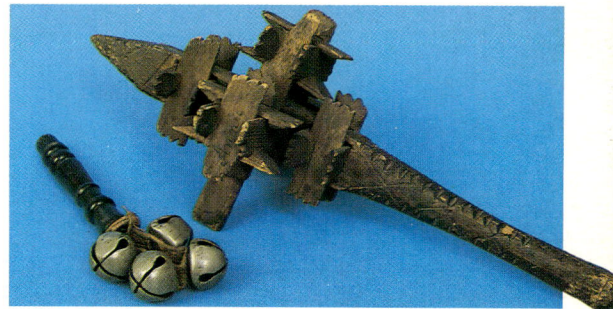

London, 1911. Children were sent out to play in the streets. This was much safer than it would be today, because almost all the traffic was horse drawn. These children have probably dressed up for the photograph.

Keeping baby clean

Most babies in poorer families were washed in tin baths like this.

By the turn of the century, people understood that dirt helped to cause illness and infection. Doctors advised regular bathing as a way of preventing disease. Dr Chavasse, who was a great believer in washing, advised mothers that:

'Cleanliness is one of the grand incentives to health. Do not be afraid of water and that in plenty, as it is one of the best strengtheners to a child's constitution'.

Mothers were recommended to use a clean sponge for the washing. The baby was patted dry with a napkin and then powdered.

A pair of ivory-handled hairbrushes.

Thermometers like this were used to test the baby's bathwater. The scale gives only a rough guide to the temperature.

An advertisement for soap at the turn of the century. The makers claimed that this soap cured wounds, ulcers, skin diseases, soreness, pimples, dandruff and baldness, as well as being suitable for washing babies!

Orphans and foundlings

During the Victorian era, the cities grew very fast. There was little town planning. New homes were built quickly and cheaply, and many people lived in dirty, overcrowded conditions. Partly because of this, the death rate of mothers and their babies was much higher than it is today. In the 1880s one in every 200 mothers died giving birth, compared to one in every 10,000 today. In 1900, 15 babies out of every hundred died at birth.

Parents didn't get any help from the government. If one parent died, the other still had to go out to work. Single parents might offer their babies for adoption in newspaper advertisements. Some women looked after a number of babies. Infants sent to these 'baby farms' were often neglected and, if money ran short, were badly fed and sometimes died.

Struggling parents might send their babies to relatives. Others had no choice but to go into a workhouse where males and females were often kept in different sections.

▲ Babies whose mothers died in childbirth might be looked after at a clinic. They spent most of their time lying on a day bed.

▼ Children in a Barnardo's home called Babies' Castle, Hawkshurst, Kent. During his life Dr Barnardo took in over 250,000 children. Barnardo's homes still look after children today.

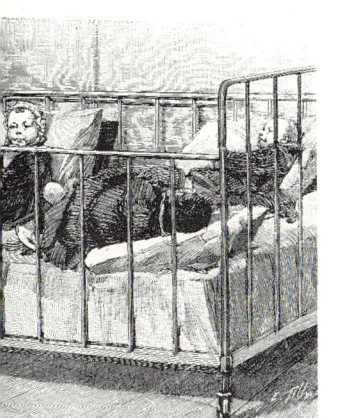

Some poor people abandoned their babies. When found, these children might be taken to a foundling hospital or to an orphanage. The babies were accepted with no questions asked, but in return the parents gave up all rights over their child.

Many orphanages contained large numbers of handicapped children. In 1905 Dr Barnardo's London homes were caring for 7,998 children, of which over 1,300 were handicapped. These children's homes received no money from the government. They were run as charities and depended on people's donations.

▼ Going to the workhouse.

Poor little mite

Babies can easily catch infant diseases, but nowadays many illnesses can be cured, or the baby can be vaccinated against them. At the turn of the century illnesses such as whooping cough, measles and scarlet fever were often fatal. Many babies, fed unsuitable food from dirty bottles or pap bowls, caught enteric fever (diarrhoea). During one summer epidemic of enteric fever in 1911, nearly 30,000 babies died.

▲ A Victorian teether. The ring is made from ivory.

▲ Woodward's Celebrated Gripe Water was first manufactured in 1851. Gripe was a word for stomach ache. Notice that alcohol is one of the ingredients.

A vaccination guard, for protecting the scab which formed after a vaccination. ▶

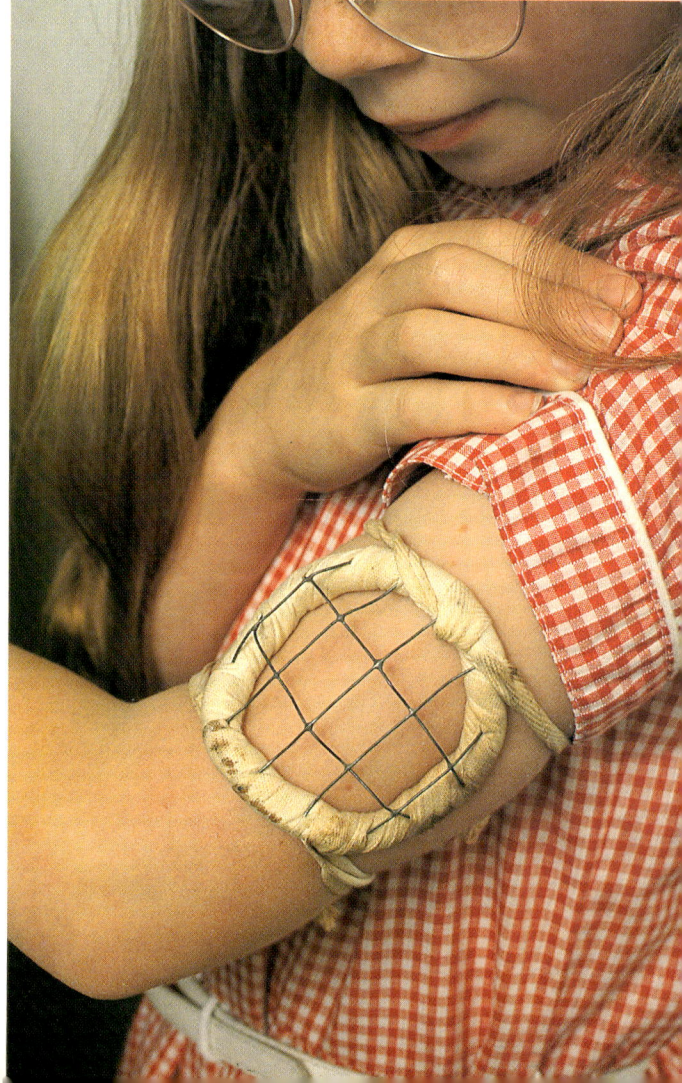

26

Doctors were expensive. Poor people called them only in a real emergency. They often prepared their own medicines, such as cough mixture made from vinegar and sugar.

All kinds of medicines were sold to cure infant diarrhoea, colic, cramps, wind or gastro-enteritis. Many of these were useless. The Victorians also believed that it was important to keep a baby's blood 'clean'. They tried to do this by dosing the children with castor oil or Epsom salts.

The unhealthy conditions in which many babies lived, combined with useless or even dangerous home cures, weakened babies and made them even more likely to catch fatal diseases. When a baby died, the parents had the added worry of paying for the funeral, which could cost 30 shillings (£1.50p), a great deal of money in those days. People who could not afford a funeral were buried in a pauper's grave. This was thought to be such a great disgrace that many poor people saved all their lives with a burial club to pay for funeral expenses.

These children visited a London cemetery. They soon found a gravestone marking the burial of a child who died aged only 3 months.

'A fit and virile race'

In 1899 the government called for volunteers to fight in the Boer War in South Africa. Out of the 12,000 men who came forward, only 1,200 were found fit enough to join the army. This alarmed the government which took some steps to improve people's health. A National Insurance scheme was introduced in 1911 to give some financial help to working men who became ill. Schools introduced lessons on housewifery and childcare.

Magazines giving advice about childcare began to appear. One of the most popular was *Baby*, a mother's magazine first published in 1907. Childcare manuals, many written by doctors, were also widely read.

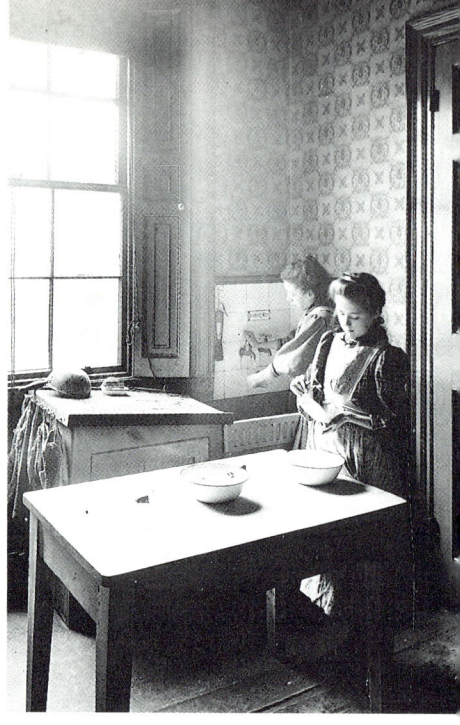

▲ Childcare classes in Barnsbury Park School, 1908. Amongst other lessons in housewifery, girls were taught how to prepare babies' bottles correctly and safely.

▼ Pages from one of Doris Cooksley's schoolbooks. These are notes she took in hygiene classes in 1910.

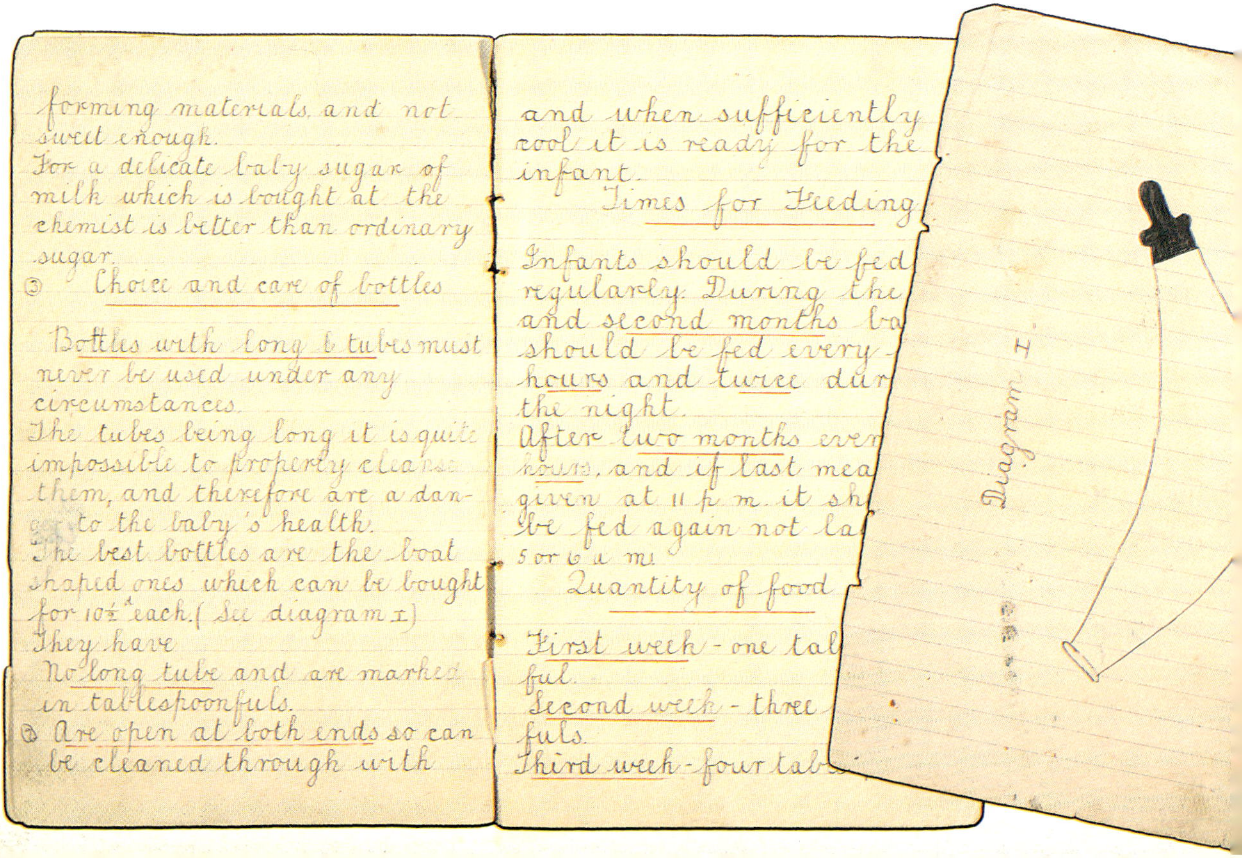

forming materials and not
sweet enough.
For a delicate baby sugar of
milk which is bought at the
chemist is better than ordinary
sugar.
③ Choice and care of bottles

Bottles with long tubes must
never be used under any
circumstances.
The tubes being long it is quite
impossible to properly cleanse
them, and therefore are a danger to the baby's health.
The best bottles are the boat
shaped ones which can be bought
for 10½d each. (See diagram I)
They have
No long tube and are marked
in tablespoonfuls.
② Are open at both ends so can
be cleaned through with

and when sufficiently
cool it is ready for the
infant.
Times for Feeding

Infants should be fed
regularly. During the
and second months ba
should be fed every
hours and twice dur
the night.
After two months ever
hours, and if last mea
given at 11 p.m. it sh
be fed again not la
5 or 6 a.m.
Quantity of food

First week - one tal
ful.
Second week - three
fuls.
Third week - four tab

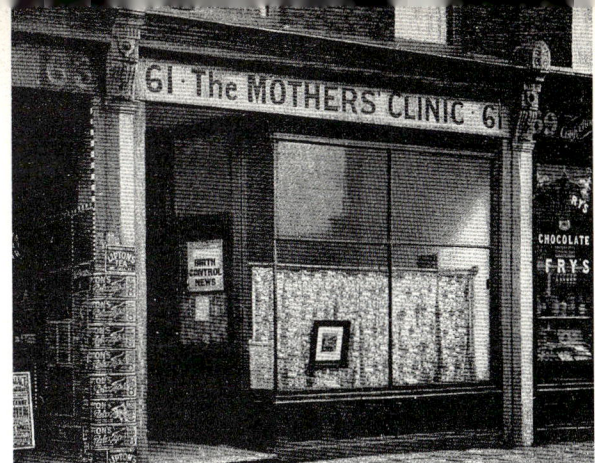

▲ The first clinics giving advice about contraception were not opened until 1921. Women who tried to publicise contraception before this time, such as Annie Besant and Marie Stopes, were criticised and even taken to court.

96 ADVICE TO A MOTHER.

SLEEP.

116. *Ought an infant's sleeping apartment to be kept warm?*

The lying-in room is generally kept *too* warm, its heat being, in many instances, more that of an oven than of a room. Such a place is most unhealthy, and is fraught with danger both to the mother and the baby. We are not, of course, to run into an opposite extreme. Keep the chamber at a moderate and comfortable temperature between 60° and 65° Fahr. The top window sash ought frequently to be let down, in order the more effectually to

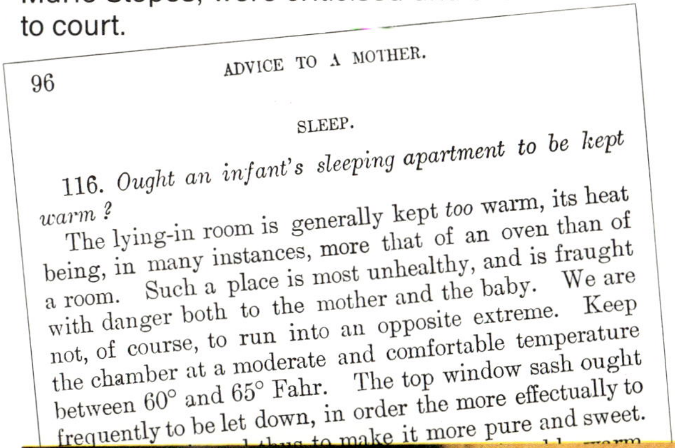

Improvements in medical treatment, such as the introduction of blood transfusions in 1914, and the training of hospital staff, especially midwives, slowly led to a reduction in the numbers of mothers and babies who died. Clinics were opened to treat infant illnesses and to teach mothers how to care for their babies. In some areas health visitors went to see mothers with new-born babies.

Although health improved after 1900, most women still knew almost nothing about family planning. Doris Cooksley remembers:

'We got lessons in childcare at school, but I didn't know anything about where babies came from, nor about childbirth until much later.'

This child compared a modern pamphlet on babycare with a manual written in 1900 (detail above). She found the old manual very hard to read.

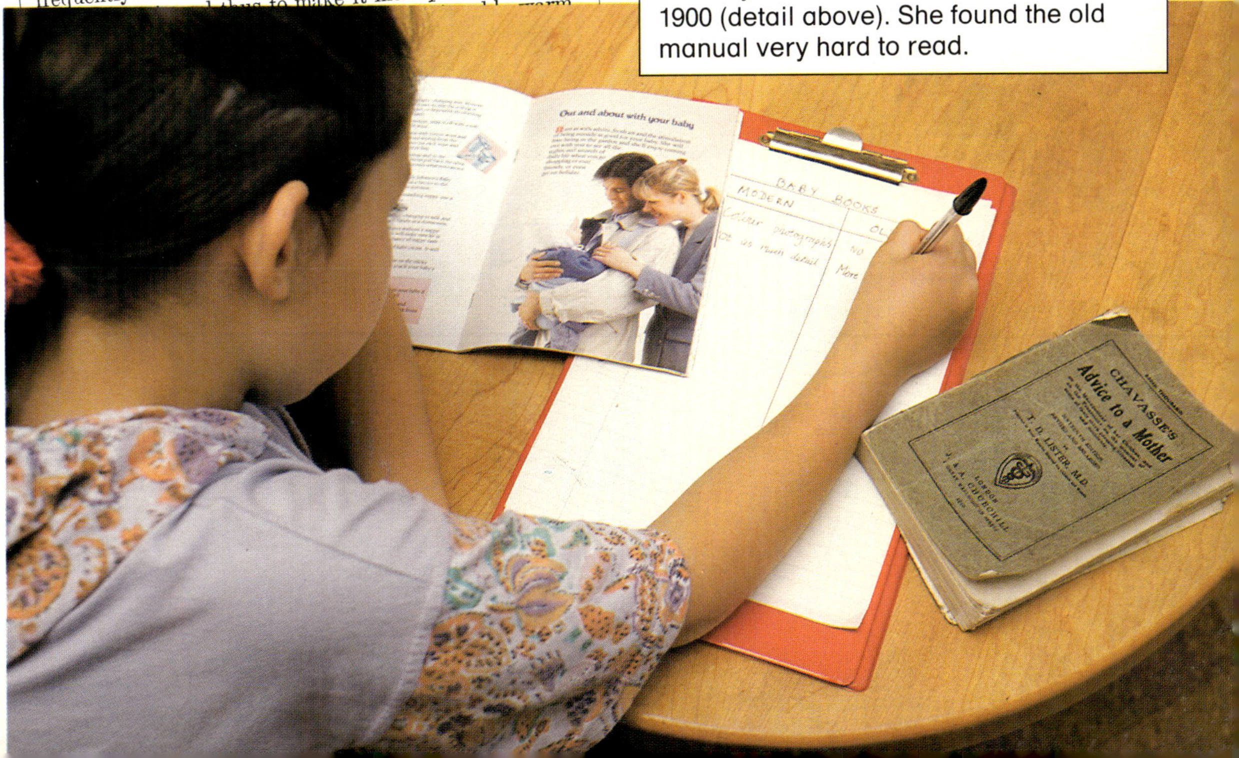

How to find out more

Start here	To find out about	Who will have
Old people	Bringing up babies at the turn of the century	Old photos, scrap books, old toys
Museums	Old things to look at and possibly to handle	Reconstructed nurseries, displays of objects connected with babies
Libraries	• Loan collections • Reference collections • Information to help your research • local history section	• Books to borrow • Books, magazines, newspapers • Useful addresses, guide books, additional reference material • Newspapers and guides to look at. Photographs of local families which include babies
Local records office	Your area in the past	Local documents, and tapes of local people talking about their childhood. Facts and figures about childhood at the turn of the century
Manufacturers of baby products	History of their products	Booklets, pictures, advertisements and information about the history of their products
Local parish church	Births, marriages and deaths	Registers of baptisms, marriages and burials. Have a look at the gravestones while you're there

Who can tell you more?

They can. Use a tape recorder for recording their memories. Handle anything they show you with great care and if they lend you something, label it with their name and keep it somewhere safe

The curator or the museum's education officer. Many museums have bookshops and a notice board where it would be worth looking for further information

- The librarian
- The reference librarian
- Ask the archivist for the name and address of the local history society

The archivist. These offices are often quite small and get very busy. Arrive early or make an appointment

The Public Relations Officer of the company, part of whose job is to help with queries like yours

The vicar. Some parish registers are kept in Public Records Offices. The vicar will be able to give you permission to check registers in the church, or tell you where the local registers can be found

Places to visit

The following places have displays, reconstructions or exhibitions connected with nurseries and babies.

Cecil Higgins Art Gallery, Castle Close, Bedford, Bedfordshire. Tel: 0234–211222.
Museum of Childhood, High Street, Edinburgh, Lothian. Tel: 031–225–1131.
Museum of Childhood, Water Street, Menai Bridge, Anglesey, Gwynedd. Tel: 0248–712498.
Museum of Childhood, Cambridge Heath Road, London. Tel: 081–980–2415.
Museum of Social History, 27 King's Street, King's Lynn, Norfolk. Tel: 0553–775004.
North of England Open Air Museum, Beamish Hall, Beamish, Stanley, Durham. Tel: 0207–31811.
Sudbury Hall, Sudbury, Derbyshire.
Tel: 028–378–305.
The Robert Opie Collection, Albert Warehouse, Gloucester Docks, Gloucester. Tel: 0452–302309

The following places have displays, reconstructions or exhibitions connected with babies' toys:

Blaise Castle House, Henbury, Bristol.
Tel: 0272–506789.
Bromsgrove Museum, 26 Birmingham Road, Bromsgrove, Hereford and Worcester.
Tel: 0527–77934.
Burrows Toy Museum, York Street, Bath.
Tel: 0225–61819.
Dolls and Miniatures, 54 Southside Street, The Barbican, Plymouth. Tel: 0752–663676.
Hamilton House Toy Museum, Church Street, Ashbourne, South Derbyshire. Tel: 0335–44343.
Pollocks Toy Museum, 1 Scala Street, London W1P 1LT. Tel: 071–636–3452.
Ribchester Dolls House and Model Museum, Church Street, Ribchester, Lancashire.
Tel: 025484–261.
Toy Museum, 42 Bridge Street Row, Chester, Merseyside. Tel: 0244–316351.
Vintage Toy and Train Museum, Sidmouth, Devon.

Index

adoption 6, 24
anaesthetics 4, 5, 7
ante-natal classes 4, 6

baby carriages 21
   prams 7, 20
   pushchairs 20
baby farms 24
Babygro suits 7
baptism 30
Barnardo's homes 24, 25
bathing 22
   soap 23
   tin baths 22
bedtime 21
Besant, Annie 29
birth 4, 5, 6, 7, 8, 9, 24
   Birth Registration Certificate 9
   childbirth 7, 9, 24, 29
   natural childbirth 7
Boer War 28
'breeching' 12

charities 25
childcare 28, 29
childcare manuals 28, 29
christening certificate 8
clinics 6, 24, 29
clothing 10, 11, 12, 18
cot 7, 19
crawling 12

death 5, 7, 8, 9, 15, 24, 26, 27, 29, 30
dirt 14, 22
diseases 14, 16, 22, 23, 26, 27
   diarrhoea 26, 27
   diphtheria 6
   enteric fever 26
   gastro-enteritis 16, 27
   measles 26
   scarlet fever 26
   smallpox 6
   tuberculosis 6
   vitamin deficiency diseases 16
   whooping cough 26
doctors 4, 5, 6, 7, 12, 20, 22, 27

family planning 7, 9, 29
feeding
   baby feeders 11
   baby food 7, 16
   breast feeding 7, 13
   condensed milk 15
   demand feeding 7
   feeding bottle 3, 6, 11, 14, 15, 18, 26, 28
   flour 15, 16
   food 6, 14, 15, 16, 19, 26
   hand feeding 15
   milk 6, 13, 14, 15, 16
   pasteurised milk 6
   sterilised milk 6, 14
   strained baby foods 7
   teats 14, 15
   tinned food 7, 15, 16
foundlings 24

germs 14, 16
gin 5
Godfrey's Cordial 17
gripe water 26

health visitor 29
hospital 4, 29
   foundling hospitals 25

incubator 4

layette 10, 11, 12

Maternity and Child Welfare Act 6

medical care 4, 9, 29
medicine 17, 27
midwife 5, 6, 29
milk steriliser 15

nanny 11, 18, 19, 20, 21
nappies 7, 10, 11
   disposable nappies 7, 10
National Society for the Prevention of Cruelty to Children 6
nurseries 6, 18, 19, 20, 30, 31
   day nursery 6, 18, 19
   night nurseries 19
   nurse-maid 18

orphanages 15, 25
orphans 24

pap 16, 26
pap boats 16
Pasteur, Louis 6
pilches 10, 11
Public Health Act 6

Queen Victoria 6, 14

rattles 21

safety pin 6, 10, 11
Spock, Doctor 7
Stopes, Marie 29

teeth 16

vaccination 6, 26
vaccination guard 26
vaccine 6
vitamins 16

weaning 16
wet-nurses 13

Acknowledgements

The author and publisher would like to thank Gill Tanner and Ruth Thomson for loaning items from their collections for photography. They would also like to thank Janet Young (Education Officer) and Andrea George (Assistant Curator) of the Cecil Higgins Art Gallery and Museum; Doris Cooksley; Suella Postles (Curator, Brewhouse Yard Museum, Nottingham); Nottingham Museum staff; Margaret Evans, Sarah Edwards and Richard Davis at *Aberystwyth Yesterday*; Chloe Inskip, Joanna Grey, Francoise Older, Simon Gibson, Krishen Bhautoo, Jonathan Bedeau, Jane and Kate Hartoch; Julie Parkin and Lesley Ely (Head) of St James V. V. Lower School, Biddenham, Bedfordshire; and Bridget Gibbs.

Photographs by Maggie Murray except for: p24 (bottom) Barnardo's; p8 (bottom), 28 (bottom) from the collection of Doris Cooksley; p9 (top), 13 (top), 17 (bottom), 24 (top), 29 (top) Mary Evans Picture Library; p13 (bottom) Chris Fairclough; p4 (Brenda Prince), 8 (top) (Judy Harrison) Format Photographers; p12 (top), 18 (right), 19 (centre) by kind permission of the Cecil Higgins Art Gallery; p1, 21 (bottom), 28 (top) Greater London Photographic Library; p26 (left) Robert Opie; p5 (bottom), 9 (bottom), 12 (bottom), 16 (left), 18 (left), 20 (right), 23 (bottom right) from the collection of Ruth Thomson.

Mrs Rene Pennington
3 Melford Drive
Billinge
Wigan
WN5 7DG

Supporting
BritishRedCross